The Paradoxical
Commandments

The Paradoxical Commandments

Finding Personal Meaning
in a Crazy World

Kent M. Keith

INNER
OCEAN

Library of Congress Cataloging-in-Publication Data

Keith, Kent M.

    The paradoxical commandments : finding personal meaning in
a crazy world / Kent M. Keith. --Makawao, Hawaii : Inner
Ocean, 2001.

    p. ; cm.

  ISBN 1-930722-05-2

    1. Conduct of life.   2. Life skills.   3. Ethics   I. Title.

BJ1581.2 .K45 2001
170--dc21   CIP

Inner Ocean Publishing, Inc.
P.O. Box 1239
Makawao, Maui, HI 96768-1239

Cover design: Bill Greaves
Cover photo: Image Bank
Interior page design: Bill Greaves
Interior page typography: Beth Hansen-Winter

Printed in Canada by Friesens

9 8 7 6 5 4 3 2 1

To my wife, Elizabeth,
and our children,
Kristina, Spencer, and Angela

Contents

Foreword

The most important thing about the Paradoxical Commandments is that they work for many people. This is especially true of their author, Kent Keith. He walks his talk. It is this authenticity that makes this so powerful for him and for all of us.

When I first met Kent, I didn't know that he had written the original ten Paradoxical Commandments, but now that I know it, I'm not surprised. In the hours that we have spent talking about life and work, he has always emphasized personal meaning, and has always been clear-headed about where to find it. As a result, he has taken on some tough, high-risk assignments. He has also had the courage to break away from some traditional patterns of life and work.

After one of our longest talks, Kent walked away from prestige, power, and money to follow his heart. He left the presidency of a university to study, think, and be with his family. He emerged with an even stronger mission and purpose. And he emerged with this book.

For years, I have encouraged Kent to devote more time to writing and speaking. Now, in this book, he shares his thoughts and experience about something he has always been good at—finding personal meaning. His book is simple, eloquent, and profound. It will touch you in surprising ways.

Most important, it will help you to live a life that is rich in personal meaning. And that, as Kent explains, is the kind of life most worth living.

Spencer Johnson, M.D.
Author, *Who Moved My Cheese?*
Co-Author, *The One Minute Manager*

Preface

I was nineteen, a sophomore at Harvard, when I wrote "The Paradoxical Commandments of Leadership." They were part of a booklet I wrote for high school student leaders entitled *The Silent Revolution: Dynamic Leadership in the Student Council*, which was published by Harvard Student Agencies in 1968. I revised the booklet and a new edition was published by the National Association of Secondary School Principals several years later. Somewhere around thirty thousand copies were sold in the late sixties and early seventies.

During the turbulent sixties, I was actively speaking at high schools, student leadership workshops, and state student council conventions in eight states. I encouraged students to work through the system to achieve change. I didn't tell them that working through the system was easy. I told them that it took sustained effort, and that the sustained effort needed to be motivated by a genuine concern for others. I stressed that point because I had seen too many students start out with high hopes and high ideals, and then give up because they got negative feedback or suffered failure. If they really cared about others, they would have the strength to keep trying, even if things were tough.

I laid down the Paradoxical Commandments as a challenge. The challenge is to always do what is right and good and true, even if others don't appreciate it. Making the world a better place can't depend on applause. You have to keep striving, no matter what, because if you don't, many of the things that need to be done in our world will never get done.

I had heard lots of excuses, and I wasn't buying them. OK—maybe people are illogical, unreasonable, and self-centered. So what? You have to love them anyway. And maybe the good you do today will be forgotten tomorrow. So what? You have to do good anyway.

The specific Commandments grew out of my own experience and observations of life. Several incidents that shaped the Commandments are described in the text. However, if there was a single experience behind the Commandments, it was the insight that I had as I walked into the stadium for the student awards ceremony at the end of my senior year at my high school. It occurred to me at that moment that I was so happy about what I had done that year, and I felt so good about what I had learned and whom I had helped, that I didn't need any awards. *I had already been rewarded.* I already had the sense of meaning and satisfaction that came from doing a good job. The meaning and satisfaction were mine, whether or not anybody gave me an award.

That realization was a major breakthrough for me. I felt completely liberated, and completely at peace. I knew that if I did what was right and good and true, my actions would have their own intrinsic value. I would always find meaning. I didn't have to have glory.

For nearly twenty-five years, I continued working, speaking, and writing without hearing anything more about the

Paradoxical Commandments. Then one day six years ago, I got a call from Honolulu Police Chief Michael Nakamura. "I was at a conference for police chiefs on the mainland," he said, "and a speaker read the 'Paradoxical Commandments of Leadership' by Kent Keith. Are *you* that Kent Keith?" I said I was. A year later, a librarian at Chaminade University showed me a printout of the Paradoxical Commandments that she had found on the Internet, where it was being distributed to librarians. Months after that, Dr. Fran Newman, a faculty member from the University of Southern California, came to Honolulu to teach a course in USC's doctoral program. She passed out the Paradoxical Commandments in class, saying that she had used the Commandments as the opening theme for every graduate class that she had taught.

In September 1997, after Mother Teresa died, I was at a meeting of my Rotary Club. It is customary to begin each meeting with a poem, prayer, or thought for the day. That day, a fellow Rotarian commented on the passing of Mother Teresa, and said he wanted to read a poem she had written. As I stood there with bowed head, I heard him read something that I recognized. I went up afterward and asked him where he had gotten it. He said it was in a book about Mother Teresa.

The next night I went to a bookstore, and started looking through the shelf of books about the life and works of Mother Teresa. There it was, on the last page before the appendices in a book entitled *Mother Teresa: A Simple Path*, compiled by Lucinda Vardey. The poem was entitled "Anyway," and it was eight of the Paradoxical Commandments that I had written and published in 1968. The words were reformatted to look like a poem, but otherwise the words were the same. There was no author listed, but at the bottom, it said: "From a sign on the wall of Shishu Bhavan, the children's home in Calcutta."

I stood there in the bookstore, chills going up and down my spine. It was an incredible moment for me. Something I had written thirty years earlier had made its way around the world to India, where Mother Teresa or one of her coworkers had thought it important enough to put up on the wall, to look at every day as they ministered to their children. I was deeply moved. I had great respect for the spirituality and work of Mother Teresa. I also knew something about children's homes, because my wife and I adopted our three children from children's homes in Japan and Romania.

A few weeks after the Rotary meeting, I dropped by to see my pastor, Rev. Don Asman, to share the news about the Paradoxical Commandments. I walked into his office and saw a copy of *Mother Teresa: A Simple Path* on his desk. He had just been given a copy. I opened the book, showed him the page, and told him the story. When I sent a copy of the book about Mother Teresa to my sister Mona in California, she passed it along to her daughter, Lisa, a teacher at a private high school. Lisa was surprised. She knew the Paradoxical Commandments. They were up on the wall in the teacher's lounge.

I was fascinated that the Paradoxical Commandments had spread around the world, and after twenty-five years they began to come back to me in various ways and shapes. It suggested to me that people today are as hungry as ever for meaning and spiritual truth. It also suggested to me that people might want to know more about the Paradoxical Commandments.

This book is for people who want to know more. It is about what the Paradoxical Commandments mean—the stories and ideas behind them, and what it means to live them. I am convinced that no matter how crazy the world is, people can find personal meaning. I am also convinced that the world would make more sense if people lived paradoxical lives, focused on personal meaning instead of recognition and applause.

I am indebted to the many people who provided their comments on drafts of this book. I want to thank Rev. Don Asman, Rev. John Bolin, SM, Dr. Lee G. Bolman, Robert R. Dye, Charles W. Filson, Lt. Col. Burke Garrett, Joe Hunt, Jasmin Iwasaki, Rev. Fred Kammer, SJ, Mildred and Richard Kosaki, Anton Krucky, Sr. Kathleen Maurice, Les and Lisa Miyamoto, Rev. Robert and Betty Morgan, Dr. Fran Newman, H.F. O'Reilly, Mona Radice, Jerry Rauckhorst, Sr. Ruth Sheehy, Dr. William G. Tierney, Jean Varney, Dr. Stephen Weiner, Linda Andrade Wheeler, Dr. Les Wilbur, Jana Wolff, Vernon Wong, and my wife, Elizabeth Keith, for their insights and encouragement.

I owe many thanks to Wally Amos for his enthusiastic support, and for putting me in touch with Inner Ocean Publishing. At Inner Ocean Publishing, I am grateful for the professionalism, creativity, energy, and sense of humor of Roger Jellinek, Bill Greaves, John Nelson, Chip McClelland, and John Elder. Finally, I want to thank Spencer Johnson. His friendship, advice, and encouragement led to the writing of this book.

Kent M. Keith
Honolulu, Hawaii
2001

The Paradoxical Commandments

Part One

It's a Crazy World

It's a Crazy World

It's best to begin by just admitting that the world is crazy. The world really doesn't make sense.

We are polluting ourselves into a corner. All of our natural systems are in decline. We are growing at a population rate the earth may not be able to support. We act as though our resources will last forever, instead of replenishing them and building a sustainable future.

While progress has been made in nuclear disarmament, there are still tens of thousands of nuclear warheads on the planet—enough to kill each man, woman, and child three or four times. As few as one hundred nuclear bombs, exploding over cities, could generate enough dark clouds to shut off our sunlight and doom all life on our planet.

There is enough food produced throughout the world to provide sufficient calories for each person on the planet. However, hundreds of thousands of people die each year of starvation, and more than a billion people on our planet are significantly undernourished.

Millions of people are suffering from diseases for which we have cures. An estimated 700 million people are infected with parasites—roundworm, hookworm, and whipworm. Poverty-stricken countries can't afford to buy vaccines to prevent polio, measles, and yellow fever, or distribute the drugs that fight tuberculosis or leprosy. Only 8 million of the 80 million children in poor countries have been immunized against diphtheria, whooping cough, and tetanus. It is estimated that 25 million people in tropical countries have become blind from diseases that were preventable.

The United States is the wealthiest nation in the world, but more than 11 million children are stuck below the poverty level. From 1980 to 1990, the number of children under age five living below the poverty level increased by 23 percent.

We say the future depends on our children, but we don't spend a lot of time with them. The time that parents spend with their children in meaningful interactions is measured in minutes per day, while television watching is measured in hours. We hope that our schools will do the job we aren't doing at home, but we pay our schoolteachers a tiny percentage of what we pay professional athletes. We graduate hundreds of thousands of students each year who cannot read their own high school diplomas.

We isolate our teenagers from the world, quarantining them in school buildings. We give them little responsibility, and demand of them even less. By cutting them off from the adult world, where they could develop a sense of competence and belonging, we leave them alienated and open to joining gangs that will give them a sense of belonging. In the 1980s it was estimated that more than 135,000 students in America carried a gun to school. The nation mourns when the alienation and weapons result in a killing spree on campus.

We are a litigious society. We file as many as 100 million lawsuits each year. Some of these are filed by individuals who

The world
doesn't make sense
but *you*
can make sense.

simply do not think they are responsible for their own actions. Even when they do wrong, they sue others, and sometimes they get rich.

Meanwhile, people who betray their spouses or children, and people who murder, steal, take drugs, or commit other outrageous acts, become television talk show guests. Some make hundreds of thousands of dollars by writing books, or selling their stories to TV, magazines, or the movies.

We want our country to be built on merit, but *who* you know is often more important than *what* you know. We say we are for equality, but racial and ethnic minorities have had to fight for an equality that has not yet been attained.

Many people have turned away from human values that have served all the generations that came before us. Some people have decided that all things are relative and subjective. They attribute no meaning to anything, and then complain that life is empty and has no meaning.

Yes, the world is crazy. If it doesn't make sense to you, you're right. *It really doesn't make sense.*

The point is not to complain about it. The point is not to give up hope. The point is this: The world doesn't make sense, but *you* can make sense. You can find personal meaning. That's what this book is about. It's about finding personal meaning in a crazy world.

Because the world is crazy and you're not, you will find personal meaning in paradox. A "paradox" is an idea that is contrary to popular opinion, something that seems to contradict common sense and yet is true. Here are ten paradoxical commandments to live by.

The Paradoxical Commandments

1. People are illogical, unreasonable, and self-centered. *Love them anyway.*

2. If you do good, people will accuse you of selfish ulterior motives. *Do good anyway.*

3. If you are successful, you will win false friends and true enemies. *Succeed anyway.*

4. The good you do today will be forgotten tomorrow. *Do good anyway.*

5. Honesty and frankness make you vulnerable. *Be honest and frank anyway.*

6. The biggest men and women with the biggest ideas can be shot down by the smallest men and women with the smallest minds. *Think big anyway.*

7. People favor underdogs but follow only top dogs. *Fight for a few underdogs anyway.*

8. What you spend years building may be destroyed overnight. *Build anyway.*

9. People really need help but may attack you if you do help them. *Help people anyway.*

10. Give the world the best you have and you'll get kicked in the teeth. *Give the world the best you have anyway.*

If you can accept the Paradoxical Commandments, then you are free. You are free from the craziness of this world. The Paradoxical Commandments can be your personal "declaration of independence." Put them up on your wall as a reminder of your freedom. For the rest of your life, you can do what you believe is right and good and true because *it makes sense to you.*

The Paradoxical Commandments are not morbid or pessimistic. If you do what is right and good and true, you will often be appreciated for your contributions. But if you can find personal meaning *without* the world's applause, you are free. You are free to do what makes sense to you, whether or not others appreciate it. You are free to be who you really are. You are free to be who you were *meant* to be. You are free to find the meaning that others miss. And when you find that meaning, you will find a happiness deeper than any you have ever known.

The Paradoxical Commandments are a call to meaning— a call to finding personal meaning in a crazy world. In this book I will explore the meaning of the Paradoxical Commandments, and then describe how to live the paradoxical life.

If you can find
personal meaning
without the
world's applause,
you are free.

Part Two

The Paradoxical
Commandments

The First Commandment

People are illogical, unreasonable,
and self-centered.
Love them anyway.

Lucy, in the *Peanuts* cartoon strip by Charles Schulz, once said: "I love mankind. It's *people* I can't stand."

People can certainly be difficult. Some are hard to love. Some are so illogical, unreasonable, and self-centered that we can't stand them. But we should love them anyway.

Love is the greatest gift that we can give and receive. It is a gift that all of us *need* to give and receive. A life without love is a life that is not fully lived. Don't limit your life by limiting your love.

The psychologist Abraham Maslow once observed that love is as essential to the growth of a human being as vitamins, minerals, and protein. I believe that human beings are built to run on love. We are designed that way. If we are not giving and receiving love, we are not operating on all our cylinders. We are not who we are supposed to be. We are not all that we can be. We are not doing all that we can do.

It is a tragedy when people decide not to love others because they don't approve of them, or they see them as illogical, or unreasonable, or self-centered, and not worthy of their love. It is a tragedy because love is not about approval or worthiness. It can't be. All of us have faults and foibles. All of us have moments of poor temper, of weakness, of temptation. All of us have done things that, afterward, we wish we

Love is the
greatest gift
that we can give
and receive.

had not done. We do not always behave in approved ways, and we are not always worthy. If approval and worthiness were really a prerequisite for love, there would be very little love in the world.

Love at its best is unconditional. We love and are loved in spite of our faults and foibles. Of course, we should strive to grow and improve. But the desire and strength to grow and improve can come from loving and being loved.

We all know people who are frustrating to be around. They have lots of needs, and they are very demanding. They often don't make sense, and are unreasonable in their attitudes. They seem so self-centered. Maybe they are. And yet, if we can love them, they may feel our love, and it may bring out the best in them. Our love can transform people and make them more lovable. As the poet Theodore Roetke said, "Love begets love."

One of my favorite movies is *African Queen* starring Humphrey Bogart and Katherine Hepburn. Bogart is rather crusty, and Hepburn is rather prissy, as they start their trip down the river on Bogart's boat. She doesn't like his drinking, and tosses his liquor bottles overboard. He doesn't like her preaching, and regrets that he ever offered to give her a ride. Gradually, however, they are caught up in their common desire to escape from the Germans. They endure hardships, they share compassion, they fall in love, and they become different people. Each of them saw the other as illogical, unreasonable, and self-centered when their trip began. That's not how they see each other when their trip ends. They beam with love as they are married by the captain of the German gunboat, just

Don't limit
your life
by limiting
your love.

before it strikes the homemade torpedo sticking out of the half-sunk *African Queen*.

Sometimes people appear to be illogical and unreasonable, when they are simply using a different logic and a different method of reasoning. They may have different worldviews, or different experiences, or see a different set of facts than we do.

There is a story I remember reading in elementary school. It is about a group of blind people standing around an elephant. One touched the elephant's trunk and announced that an elephant is like a hose. Another put his arms around the elephant's leg and said that an elephant is like a tree trunk. Another placed his hands on the elephant's side and said that an elephant is like a wall. Another grasped the elephant's tail and announced that an elephant is like a rope. And so it went. Each person was right, and each person was wrong. They were right about the parts they touched, but wrong because they didn't see the whole picture. It was not until all the parts were put together that a true picture of an elephant emerged.

Ever since reading that story, I have tried to remember that some of the "illogical and unreasonable" people in the world simply have their hands on different parts of the elephant than I do. Another simple saying is that "there are three answers to every question: Yours, mine, and the right one."

So enjoy the immense personal meaning that comes from giving and receiving the gift of love. Love is too important to miss, just because others are "difficult." Often, they are no more difficult than you or I!

People are illogical, unreasonable, and self-centered.
Love them anyway.

The Second Commandment

*If you do good, people will accuse
you of selfish ulterior motives.
Do good anyway.*

I learned this commandment when I was fifteen, a sophomore in high school.

I was interested in student government. At my high school, there was a representative assembly which consisted of an elected representative from each home room. The student body officers presided over meetings of the representative assembly. Each grade level had its own class officers as well, who met to plan class activities like the junior prom.

In the fall of my sophomore year, the student body officers decided that they would like to get rid of the representative assembly and form a smaller council consisting of the class officers and the student body officers. They said that this would unify the class councils and the student body government and make things more efficient. They sincerely believed that this would be a major improvement.

Their reorganization plan disturbed me. The representative assembly was a broad-based group with about sixty-five members. The new council would have only twenty members. To me, the representative assembly stood for grassroots student involvement and democracy. The new council would reduce the number of student participants by more than two-thirds. I thought it would be an elitist group, a kind of oligarchy. Twenty students would represent twenty-four hundred students.

Since the reorganization would require a school-wide vote to change the student government constitution, the campus leaders began talking it up. When they presented their plan, I spoke up against it. When the student body president did a public announcement supporting the plan, I asked for—and was given—equal time for rebuttal. When the school paper published an editorial supporting the reorganization, I wrote a letter criticizing it. For weeks, I was the only student who was willing to publicly oppose the new plan.

My criticisms irritated the campus leaders. They were the "in" crowd, the social leaders of the campus, and they were not used to being opposed. I had to live with their jeers, their snide remarks, their insults. They got my class schedule, and twice they came into the class I was attending, telling the teacher that they wanted to debate me then and there, with no warning. Once, the teacher let them. Some of the supporters of the reorganization even picketed during lunchtime. The signs they held as they circled in front of the school not only supported the reorganization, but attacked me personally. I was persona non grata in all the "right" circles.

After a few weeks, five or six other students decided to publicly oppose the plan. Awareness of the issue on campus grew. Finally, it was agreed that we would have a debate at a school assembly before the student body voted on the issue. Two tables were set up on the stage in the auditorium, with several student speakers at each. I led the speakers at the opposition table. The assembly lasted less than an hour, but it was enough time to get our points across.

When the vote was taken, the reorganization was defeated

by a vote of seventeen hundred to four hundred. We won an astounding victory. The representative assembly was not abolished, and the smaller council was not established. Months later, the student body president told me that the reorganization plan had been a mistake, and she was glad it failed.

I thought it took courage to take on the campus leaders as a new sophomore in my second month at the school. Those first few weeks, during which I was the only voice of opposition, were very lonely ones. I did not enjoy being attacked, and I could not believe I was being picketed. I was made to feel like an outcast, and it was not a good feeling.

After we won, I was elated. The vote made it clear that I was not alone, that in fact 80 percent of the student body understood what I was trying to say. I decided to get more involved. The following spring, I signed up to run for student body vice president. When the list of candidates came out with my name on it, one of the campus leaders got in his last snide remark. "I knew it," he said. "You just opposed the reorganization as a way of getting your name out front, so you could run for office. You're just an opportunist." He made a face and walked away.

I was stunned. When I opposed the reorganization, I was certain that I was giving up any possibility of being elected or appointed to *anything*. I was an object of contempt among the campus leaders. And I didn't expect to win. I felt strongly about the issue, so I decided to speak up. Now, the stand I took was being characterized as a public relations stunt, a calculated move by a political opportunist. I couldn't believe that anybody would think that, much less say that.

People who act on
their own selfish motives
commonly accuse others
of doing the same thing.

I have seen this happen over and over again. People who are twisted and bent, cynical and tired, have usually given up doing good. Instead, they are just trying to get what they can for themselves. They justify their behavior by claiming that everybody else is the same—everybody else is just out for themselves, too. They attribute their own motives to others. People who are doing good are seen as people who are only *pretending* to be doing good, when in fact they are after something selfish.

In short, people who act on their own selfish ulterior motives commonly accuse others of doing the same thing. So if you do good, what you have done may be belittled in the eyes of the twisted and bent, the cynical and tired. That is sad, but it says more about them than about you. You still need to do what is right and good and true. That is where the personal meaning and satisfaction are to be found.

> *If you do good, people will accuse you*
> *of selfish ulterior motives. Do good anyway.*

The Third Commandment

*If you are successful, you will win false
friends and true enemies.
Succeed anyway.*

When I became the director of a state government agency
and a member of the governor's cabinet, I was startled to discover how many new friends I suddenly had. Business and
community leaders were available when I wanted to see them;
in fact, some wanted to see *me*, to ask me to support their
projects and ideas. I was invited to give speeches at hundreds
of conferences and special events. I sat at head tables. Report-
ers called regularly. I was in the newspaper every few weeks
and on TV or radio at least once a month. I had a lot of new
friends.

I also had a lot of new enemies. Actually, they weren't *my*
enemies, but they saw me as *their* enemy. This was hard to
fathom, since I had never attacked them—in fact, I didn't even
know them. They decided to attack me as a way of attacking
the governor, or my political party, or the government in general. They attacked me for saying things I had never said, and
for doing things I had never done.

There were people within my department who would
pretend to be friendly and supportive, but who were quietly
working to get me ousted. They didn't like the direction in
which I wanted the department to go. They liked things the
way they were. I wanted to build a shared management team,
but they wanted to continue to rule their independent king-

doms. It was a difficult period of establishing new goals, processes, and relationships.

By the time the governor's term was over and my commission as a department head expired, I had come to truly enjoy the business and community leaders I worked with and felt a new sense of camaraderie and teamwork within the department. I was proud of what we had accomplished, and I liked the people with whom I worked.

The day I left office, however, most of my relationships changed. I took an exciting new job in business, but I was not a CEO. I was a project manager, several levels lower than a CEO. It was a great job, but I was no longer "important." I no longer had "status." People I had worked with closely now seemed a little embarrassed to bump into me on the street. *They* were still movers and shakers, but I wasn't. I wasn't getting invitations, my support was no longer being sought, the press wasn't calling for interviews.

This cycle of suddenly acquiring friends and enemies, and then just as suddenly losing them, is a cycle I have experienced more than once. I know it has happened to thousands of other people. I was not surprised or disillusioned. Fortunately, when I first became the director of the department, a mentor had told me to remember, every day, that I would not always be the director. I would not always be in the public limelight. I would not always be in a position of influence. I should do the job knowing that the years would pass quickly, and then I would be in a new role, probably one with less power and visibility. It was like the old saying that you should be kind to the people you meet on the way up, because they are the same people you will be seeing again on your way down.

People who become "successful" learn that they have "personal" friends and "positional" friends. A personal friend is with you through thick and thin, high position, low position, or no position. A personal friend truly cares about you and enjoys your company.

A "positional" friend is a friend of your position of power or influence. He was the friend of the last person to have your position, and he will be the friend of the next person to have your position. This is good for business. It maintains networks that are useful to both you and to the positional friend. There is nothing wrong with this. You just have to remember to not confuse positional friends with personal ones. Positional friends are not "true" friends in the usual sense of the word.

When they retire or leave their positions, government leaders, military generals, and big company CEOs discover a change in their positional friends. Suddenly, their positional friends are too busy to meet them for lunch. Their positional friends don't return their phone calls anymore. Their positional friends don't laugh at their jokes or admire their ideas anymore. The reason is simple: Their positional friends are now focused on the new government official, the new general, the new CEO. They have new lunches to go to, new phone calls to answer, new jokes to laugh at, new ideas to admire.

Then, of course, there are the really false friends—people who want to use you and your position for their own ends, in the most crass sense. Unlike positional friends, who want to maintain a good relationship while you have your position, false friends are just pretending, waiting for the right moment to make use of you and then turn and run.

Even worse, when you are successful, you win true enemies. Somebody else wanted your success. Somebody else lost when you won. Somebody doesn't want your star to rise because he sees himself as your rival. Somebody is embittered by *anyone* who succeeds and looks for ways to attack or at least embarrass the successful. The higher you go in your organization or field of work, the easier a target you become.

There are some simple ways to handle enemies. First, don't take their behavior personally. The people who attack you may be struggling with their unhappiness at the way their own lives have turned out. They are disappointed, and blame you for their disappointment. You may be no more than a symbol to them, a convenient target available for attack. The attack really isn't about you—it's about them. You shouldn't take it personally. You should take it with patience and compassion.

Second, when other people see you as *their* enemy, you do not have to see them as *your* enemies. Some people attack because they crave more attention for themselves, and attacking you is one way to get it. Others attack because they are passionate about their beliefs and are upset that you don't see things the same way. Stay open-minded, treat your attackers fairly, listen to what they say, and give them your attention whenever it is appropriate. You may learn something. Most important, if you do not treat them as your enemies, you make it easier for them to someday become your allies and friends.

Treasure your family
and longtime friends
with whom you shared
joys and sorrows
before you were
a "success."

Finally, treasure your family and your longtime friends, the people with whom you shared joys and sorrows before you were a "success." Your family loves you for who you are, and your longtime friends didn't become your friends because of your power or position. You have things in common that make the friendship a lasting one.

My children sing a little song they were taught in school: "Make new friends, but keep the old. One is silver and the other, gold." As you go through life, as you succeed, your old friends will mean more and more to you. You will also have the opportunity to make new friends who will become true friends, new "silver" that will someday become gold.

Work hard, with vision and skill. Don't shy away from success. When the attacks come, treat your attackers with patience and compassion, and treat enemies as potential allies and friends. Most important, make sure you stay close to your *true* friends. If you do, you will find personal meaning regardless of how many false friends or true enemies come knocking at your door.

> *If you are successful, you will win false friends*
> *and true enemies. Succeed anyway.*

The Fourth Commandment

The good you do today will be
forgotten tomorrow.
Do good anyway.

I remember reading a story in elementary school about a young Egyptian foreman who was supervising the laying of the foundation for one of the pharaoh's pyramids. The foreman was out in the hot sun, encouraging, watching, correcting the work. Whenever he found that the massive stones did not fit perfectly, he would have them realigned until they were just right.

Another foreman watched him, and finally came over to give him some advice. "The foundation will all be under the ground. Nobody will see it," he said, shaking his head. "Don't worry about it. Nobody will know."

"*I* will know," the young foreman replied, continuing his work.

When you do what is right and good and true, *you* will know, and *you* will remember. That will give you all the personal meaning you need.

Yes, some of the good that you do will be recognized, but even good work that is recognized will often be forgotten. What is important is not whether anyone remembers. What is important is who you are as a person. What matters is how you live. If you are living authentically and generously, you won't worry about whether anybody else knows or remembers.

That's why the good that you do can be anonymous. Just

The good you do
may never be noticed
by others.
But *you* will know.

doing good is enough. Just knowing that you have helped somebody, or improved your organization, is enough.

That's why it doesn't matter if the good you do is credited to your successor. This is a common occurrence in organizations. A manager may work hard to lay the foundation for the future success of her department or company. Without that foundation, the future success will not occur—but when it does occur, it will most likely be after the department head or CEO has left or retired, so that the success will be credited to her successor.

When you lay the foundation for the future of your organization, *you* will know the good that you have done. You can also find great satisfaction in seeing the eventual success, even if you have retired or gone on to other things.

The fact is that some of the foundations for your own success were laid by your predecessors. That was their gift to you. The way to return that gift is to pass it on—to work hard so that you have a gift to give to the next person who will fill your shoes.

Many of the best things we can do for each other are little things that bring a smile, or lift the spirits, as we go through daily life together. Sometimes, doing good is about common courtesy and thoughtfulness.

Robbie Alm has been a successful attorney, government official, and banker in Honolulu. He and a group of friends gathered one day to think about how to make life in our community more thoughtful and civil. They developed the "Live Aloha" program. "Aloha" has many meanings, but they were thinking of it in terms of caring, affection, and courtesy. While

Who you are
and how you live
are more important
than who remembers
what you did.

there are many ways to live aloha, they felt that one way was to be courteous and civil in daily life, including doing the little things that add up and improve the quality of our lives. Here is their list of examples:

Respect your elders and children.

Leave places better than you found them.

Hold the door.

Hold the elevator.

Plant something.

Drive with courtesy. Let others in.

Attend an event of another culture.

Return your shopping cart.

Get out and enjoy nature.

Pick up litter.

Share with your neighbors.

Create smiles.

The Live Aloha group says that you don't have to be a politician, or the president of a company, or a famous doctor, to make everyone's life better. Sometimes the smallest things make the biggest difference.

So take the time to smile at the lady at the newsstand; help people carry their packages into the building; be the first to start folding up the chairs after the church meeting. Nobody may notice; nobody who notices may remember. But you will be making their lives happier in little ways that add up.

Do good for its own sake. Do good because it is part of who you are, part of your quality of life. The good you do will be a source of personal meaning for you, even if nobody knows, or those who know forget.

The good you do today will be forgotten tomorrow.
Do good anyway.

The Fifth Commandment

Honesty and frankness make
you vulnerable.
Be honest and frank anyway.

I was at a university in the Midwest during the sixties, serving as a staff member at a summer workshop for high school student council leaders. The students were divided into groups, and I was a counselor working with one of the groups. I was the youngest counselor they had ever hired. Perhaps because of that, the director of the workshop asked me to address all the students at an evening assembly.

As the day of my speech approached, the director became more nervous. He dropped by to chat with me and joked about what my speech would be about. He wanted to know what I was going to say. I told him honestly that I was still thinking about it. That seemed to make him *more* nervous.

Finally, he came to the point. He didn't want me stirring up the kids. He didn't want me doing an "activist" thing. He didn't want me attacking "the establishment." That wouldn't be good for my future there at the workshop. He wanted me to say something "nice." That was why he had asked me to speak in the first place.

The night came, and I stood at the front of the auditorium, behind the large wooden podium, looking out at hundreds of students. Some of them were talking, some were slumped down in their chairs, some were shifting restlessly. At the back of the auditorium, sitting in two rows like a human wall, were the adults—the teachers and counselors who were responsible for the student councils at their schools.

I had made my decision. I had decided not to attack the teachers or counselors or their "establishment." I had decided to do something more important. I had decided to tell the students what I really thought about their student councils. I had decided to challenge them. I had decided to be honest and frank with them.

I told them that too many of their student councils were self-congratulatory cliques, focused only on themselves, busy building their resumes for college application forms. I said they took the easy way out, and just did the same activities year after year, whether anybody else wanted those activities or not. I said that too many of them did not care about the rest of the student body—the students who elected them. I urged them to reach out, to listen to their fellow students, and work through the system to find ways to make things better for everyone. I basically told them that they were frauds, but they didn't have to be. They could make a difference in the quality of education, and the quality of life, at their schools.

When I finished half an hour later, there was silence. Then, as I said thank-you and gathered up my note cards, the applause began to grow. I had broken through the "nice-nice" environment of polite pretending. I had looked them in the eye and told them to do something more important than hold parties for themselves. And they had gotten the message.

They began to come forward, down the aisle, and up on the stage. They lifted me on their shoulders and carried me outside. It was exhilarating. We talked, and we were honest when we talked. We could *do* more. We could *be* more. We could stand for something more important than the selection of the theme song for the prom.

We talked, and then one by one, the students shook my hand and wandered back toward their dorms for the night. As they left, I began to walk back to my room. Suddenly, I was surrounded by four men. One of them was the director of the workshop. He told me I was fired, and he was there to make sure that I would be leaving immediately.

They escorted me to my room, closed and blocked the door, and told me to pack. They would not allow me to make any phone calls. They would not allow me to leave any messages. I told them that I had loaned out some personal books and materials to some of the students in my group, and I would like to get them back. They didn't say anything.

When I was packed, they escorted me to the parking lot and put me into the back of a station wagon. The driver did not turn on the car's headlights, perhaps to avoid attention as we pulled out of the parking lot. Twenty miles from the campus, they dropped me off at a roadside bus stop—an open shelter with a bench. It was 9:30 at night. I sat alone in the dark, watching the splashes of light from the headlights of the passing cars. I was eighteen years old, and I had just learned something.

What I learned was that we connected, the students and I, because we decided to be honest and frank with each other. We stopped pretending and started communicating. That honesty and frankness frightened the adults, who wanted the pretending to continue. What I said made me vulnerable, and

I was literally run out of town. But I didn't regret it. The time we spent connecting was electric.

When I think of great men and women, I often think of their honesty and frankness. It is their honesty and frankness that make it easy for me to admire them and trust them. George Washington's honesty was the stuff of legends, and Abraham Lincoln was "Honest Abe." Perhaps the thing we like best about Harry Truman is that he told it like it was.

When we are honest and frank with each other, we can build strong relationships. We know where we stand. We know how to meet each other's needs, and how to fulfill each other's dreams. Without that, we blunder and unintentionally hurt ourselves and others.

One of the most important issues in family and organizational life is trust. You don't build trust by hiding your feelings, your thoughts, your hopes, your fears. You build trust by sharing, by being honest and frank. Building trust is something you must do if you are to have successful relationships, teams, organizations, and communities.

Yes, it is important to be tactful. There are right and wrong times to say certain things, and some things shouldn't be said at all. Confidentiality is part of a trusting relationship. Some things are appropriate to share with only one person, or only a few. But tact and confidentiality should not prevent you from being honest and frank in most of your daily relationships.

Of course, being honest and frank makes you vulnerable. You show your hand. That means that it is easier for people to figure out how to attack and hurt you. When you step out from behind your defenses, you are exposed. This is not only true in intimate relationships, but also in groups and organizations.

But vulnerability can be good. When you are vulnerable, it is easier to connect with people, get to know them, and learn from them. And they will find it easier to connect with you. Vulnerability is a door to new relationships, new opportunities, new ways to grow, new ways to live and work together.

In a world of conflict, it is tempting to build up one's defenses and go around in a suit of armor. But there is a problem with that. A suit of armor protects you by *containing* you. You can only grow so much, and then you have to get out of your armor if you want to grow any further.

Once out of your armor, you will be vulnerable, but with that vulnerability comes the freedom to grow. As you enjoy personal and professional growth, you will discover that you don't need armor any more. Your strength will come from inside.

So do your best to be honest and frank. It will make you vulnerable, but that vulnerability will make it easier to connect with others, and to grow both personally and professionally. Get out of your armor and enjoy the meaning and satisfaction that come from being honest and frank.

> *Honesty and frankness make you vulnerable.*
> *Be honest and frank anyway.*

You have to
take off your armor
if you want to grow.

The Sixth Commandment

*The biggest men and women with
the biggest ideas can be shot down
by the smallest men and women
with the smallest minds.*
Think big anyway.

Socrates ... Galileo ... Joan of Arc ... Columbus ... Lincoln
... Susan B. Anthony ... Gandhi ... Martin Luther King, Jr. Our
history books are full of the stories of big men and women,
with big ideas, who were shot down—literally or figura-
tively—by smaller people. Smaller people laughed at them,
locked them up, or gunned them down.

The world needs big people, people who are generous,
principled, committed, and open to thinking and acting in
new ways to solve problems and seize opportunities. The
world also needs big ideas, ideas that will really make a difference, ideas that will generate breakthroughs, ideas that will
provoke paradigm shifts. We have big problems, and we need
big solutions. We need people who can see a better world
beyond the status quo.

But big men and women with big ideas are threatening
to small men and women with small minds. A "small person" is not a person who has a low position or title, or little
money, or little education. A "small person" is often a good
person, a hard worker committed to the organization, and a
good friend to his or her colleagues. What makes the person
a "small person" is simply that he or she sees life in very

We have
big problems.
We need
big solutions.

small terms. A small person doesn't see very far beyond his own life, his own organization, his own place and time. He has usually mastered his daily routine and doesn't want it to change. He thus clings to the way things have always been, rather than the *reason* they have always been that way. A small person wants everything nailed down and categorized, with permission forms filled out in triplicate. He doesn't want to talk about how things might be better, because then things would be different, and he doesn't want to try anything new.

A small person often sees things in terms of his or her own power, or comfort, or convenience, and believes that what is best for him is best for the family, or organization, or community. A small person's life may be no bigger than his immediate wants, needs, and fears. One thing is certain: A small person with small ideas won't lead us to new levels of excellence or an improved quality of life.

There are a hundred times more small people than big people in the world. They are everywhere, at every level of society, in every kind of business and government and nonprofit organization. Wherever they are, they do their best to shoot down big people with big visions, big dreams, big perspectives.

This is sad, because all of us, including the small people, ultimately benefit by the big ideas. We all benefit when problems are solved, deadlocks are broken, new products are invented, new ways of living are developed. Everyone benefits when a big vision, a big dream, or a big perspective opens up new opportunities and leads to desirable new realities. But small people cannot see the larger good that may come; they cling to the smaller good that they have now.

Certainly, some big ideas have generated big failures. Some big visions have been big-time flops. But often, we don't know what will work until we give it a try—an honest try, an intelligent effort with sufficient time and resources, not a grudging, foot-dragging, reluctant effort.

People and organizations need dreams. One of the functions of leadership is to formulate and articulate the mission and the vision of the group or organization. The vision is an idea about the future, an idea about what could be, what *should* be, for the organization and the people it serves. Big visions attract big people, ready to be challenged, ready to learn and grow and enhance their performance. People want to make a difference; people need a reason to hope, a goal to work toward. Small ideas don't bring out our best. Big ideas do.

There is a long list of big ideas that have changed the world and the way we live. The founding fathers of the United States dreamed of independence and a democratic republic, and gave birth to a country that has had an impact on every corner of the world. Susan B. Anthony dreamed of the day when women in America would be allowed to vote, and helped to achieve this first step in gender equality. Gandhi dreamed of freedom for India, and led a peaceful revolution that liberated 100 million people. Martin Luther King dreamed of racial equality, a dream that still calls us to justice and freedom for all.

Florence Nightingale had a vision of modern hospitals served by well-trained nurses, and in pursuing that vision,

Small ideas
don't bring out
our best.
Big ideas do.

she established the modern nursing profession and saved thousands of lives. Thomas Alva Edison had big ideas that led to the electric light and the phonograph, both of which changed lives throughout the world. Jonas Salk dreamed that polio could be stopped. He developed a vaccine that has saved millions from that disabling disease.

Eiichi Shibusawa of Japan lived from 1840 to 1931. Born into the peasant class, he rose to become a member of the elite Ministry of Finance, and then left to become an entrepreneur. He knew that Japan could not grow economically without new businesses, so he set to work creating them. During his lifetime he founded and developed more than six hundred industrial companies. He knew the importance of maximizing talent, so he served as an unofficial management counselor, organized training programs, and helped establish a famous university of economics.

Ray Kroc saw the little restaurant run by the McDonald brothers as the prototype for the modern fast-food restaurant. He turned that prototype into an international food chain with thousands of outlets and billions in revenues. Debbi Fields was a young mother with no business experience when she dreamed that she could make a success of a store that sold only cookies. Twenty years later she had more than seven hundred stores in the United States and eleven foreign countries.

Frederick W. Smith had a vision of a new kind of express delivery service. He built FedEx into an international, multibillion-dollar company with more than six hundred aircraft, sixty-one thousand vehicles, 190,000 employees, and an average volume of three million packages delivered each day throughout the world.

George Williams was a young man working as a sales assistant in a draper's shop in London in 1844. Young men like himself typically worked 10-12 hours per day, six days a week. They slept in crowded rooms over their workplaces. Williams was disturbed that young men like himself who had come to London to work had no positive alternative to life on the streets. He and a group of fellow drapers formed a Christian fellowship of young men who would help each other learn and grow in mind and spirit. His idea grew until, a century-and-a-half later, it serves thirty million men, women, and children in hundreds of programs in 130 countries—the YMCA.

Chicago lawyer Paul Harris had a big idea. In 1905 he brought together three friends and proposed to start a club that would foster fellowship among members of the business community. The idea took hold, and today there are 1.2 million business and professional leaders in twenty-nine thousand Rotary Clubs in 161 countries, enjoying fellowship and working together in service to humanity.

In 1976, Millard and Linda Fuller had a big idea called Habitat for Humanity. Quitting their jobs, the Fullers set out to make housing available to people who never dreamed they would be able to have their own homes. In less than twenty-five years, Habitat for Humanity has built more than eighty-five thousand houses around the world, providing 425,000 people in two thousand communities with safe, affordable places to live.

Dr. Ramon K. Sy and six other doctors of Filipino ancestry who lived in Hawaii went to the Philippines in 1983 to help the countrymen they had left behind. This small group had an idea that became the Aloha Medical Mission, an organization of six hundred volunteers who have performed surgical operations and given medical assistance to more than sixty-thousand people in the Philippines, China, Vietnam, Vanuatu, Bangladesh, Cambodia, and Laos as well as Hawaii.

Big ideas have established freedom, saved lives, protected the natural environment, provided new services, created jobs, and built communities. Big ideas have made a big difference. They have enhanced the quality of life for hundreds of millions of people.

Having a big idea—a dream—will make your life more meaningful. It will give you a focus, a direction. It will give you something to strive for. If your big idea is shot down, simply pick it up, dust it off, and get moving again. Every step toward the fulfillment of your dream will bring immense meaning and satisfaction.

The biggest men and women with the biggest ideas
can be shot down by the smallest men and women with
the smallest minds. Think big anyway.

The Seventh Commandment

People favor underdogs but
follow only top dogs.
Fight for a few underdogs anyway.

In 1945, at the end of World War II, a captain in the U.S.
Marine Corps landed in Tsingtao, China. There weren't many
Americans around, so he bunked at a local hotel and took his
meals with the Nationalist Chinese general who was the leader
of the Chinese bandits outside of Tsingtao. The marine
captain's assignment was to assist in the arrangements for
the surrender of Japanese forces in northern China. His first
task was to recruit dock workers to unload transports and
secure housing for the marines who would be arriving soon.

It was a time of transition from war to peace, from combat and field conditions to office and barracks duty. Some of
the marines who arrived in Tsingtao had spent their careers
in combat, and had no experience with barracks duty. One of
these, a young, newly promoted marine sergeant, was as-
signed duty as sergeant of the guard at the barracks in
Tsingtao. In that role, he signed for thirty-five alpaca vests,
accepting them as part of the guard property. When relieved
of duty the next day, only two of the vests could be located.
Winter was approaching, living quarters were not heated, and
the vests were prized possessions. Thirty-three vests had disappeared.

About the same time that the sergeant was signing for
the vests, Marine Corps headquarters issued an order requir-

ing strict property accounting. For the previous two years, there had been little or no accounting. The marines were too busy fighting the war to worry about inventories and forms. But now, it was peace time, new orders were in effect, and the sergeant was brought up on a court martial for the missing vests.

The captain agreed to serve as defense counsel for the sergeant in the general court martial case. The captain began investigating, and determined that he would have to call to the stand the regimental adjutant, the battery commander, several officers of the day, several sergeants of the guard, the regimental executive, and the regimental commander. He would have to call them because they were on-site or in command before, during, and after the jackets disappeared. Calling them to the stand would have put each of them in the court martial record, which would go to Marine Corps headquarters in Washington, DC, for review.

This was a sensitive time for the officers in the chain of command. Many were reservists who were seeking regular commissions after the war; others were seeking duty assignments that would advance their careers. The captain began to receive phone calls from these officers, asking why he was going to such lengths on behalf of a buck sergeant. The captain was called in to talk with the regimental adjutant, then the regimental executive, and then the regimental commander, all three of whom outranked him. Each of the three men "suggested" that it would be best for all concerned, certainly for the captain, if the captain did not call them as witnesses.

The captain was a reservist, and he wanted a career in the

Marine Corps. It was clear to him that upsetting his senior officers was not the way to get a regular commission and continue his career. But he was not deterred. He informed his superior officers that he would have to call them to the stand to establish the facts of the case.

The pressure increased. The marine division threw a party one Saturday night at a hotel and the captain was invited to attend. Once he got there, he was asked to come in and say hello to the assistant division commander. The assistant division commander talked about the upcoming court martial and said that he was personally worried about the captain's actions, and how they might affect his request for a regular commission. The assistant division commander mentioned that his boss, the division commander, "was being kept informed." Following that encounter, the battalion commander also visited the captain to suggest that he "ease off."

The captain listened politely to each of them. He knew his career was on the line, but he didn't think the sergeant was guilty, and he didn't think it was fair for the sergeant to take the fall. Again, he had a decision to make, and he made it. He told the assistant division commander and the battalion commander that he couldn't ease off.

Monday afternoon, the next regular training day, the sergeant came running to the captain's office with astonishing news. He had just come from the barracks, where he had found thirty-three alpaca vests on his bunk. They weren't Marine Corps vests, but U.S. Navy vests, apparently secured from navy ships in the area. Together, the captain and the sergeant took the vests over to the office of the sergeant of the guard and got a signed receipt. The sergeant of the guard notified the regimental adjutant that the vests had been located and accounted for. The following day, the captain and sergeant received word that the court martial would not be held, and all charges had been dropped.

The sergeant was promoted again before leaving the Marine Corps a few years later with an honorable discharge. The captain who risked his career to fight for an underdog received the regular commission he sought and rose through the ranks to become a colonel, serving with distinction for thirty years.

Seven or eight years after the Tsingtao court martial incident, the captain was selected to work closely with the man who had been the division commander who "was being kept informed" about the court martial. That division commander had become the commandant—the commanding general of the Marine Corps. The commandant wanted somebody he could trust. He knew he could trust the captain.

The story had a happy ending, but the courage and the risk were real. I happen to know this story because I know the man who had the courage to take the risk. He is my father.

We sympathize with underdogs. We identify with them. We love stories in which the underdogs win against the odds. We enjoy cheering for them.

But when it is our own family, our own career, our own reputation that is at stake, we usually don't take the risk. The odds are against the underdog; he or she is likely to lose. Even if the underdog is right, and in our hearts we support him, to support the underdog is to risk failure, disapproval, even the end of a job or the end of one's hopes for promotion or success in one's career. So we love the underdog, but we tend to follow the top dogs. We jump on the bandwagon, we do what is respectable. We comply. We nod. We go along.

Not every underdog is right, and not every underdog's issues are important. But some are. From time to time you will discover an underdog who needs the kind of help you can give. Because of who you are, and what you believe, you should give that help. When you look back at the end of your life, you may conclude that fighting for a few underdogs was one of the most meaningful things you ever did.

People favor underdogs, but follow only top dogs.
Fight for a few underdogs anyway.

The Eighth Commandment

What you spend years building
may be destroyed overnight.
Build anyway.

Unfortunately, it happens every day. A house burns down. A business goes bust. A fortune is lost. A flood wipes out a community. Day after day, tragedy strikes, and the things that people have spent years building are suddenly destroyed. We admire the courage that so many people exhibit in responding to these tragedies. Our hearts go out to them. We know that the pain is deep.

It is a harsh fact that the things you build may be destroyed during your lifetime. You may lose them overnight. Even if they last beyond your lifetime, they will eventually be lost.

Still, it is worth building. The act of building brings joy and satisfaction.

One of my wife's favorite memories is an afternoon she spent at the beach with our daughter, who was then four years old. Instead of building a sand castle, they decided to sculpture a turtle in the sand. They built a large one, complete with markings on his shell, cute little legs, and a very knowing look in his eyes. As they worked, the waves reached farther and farther up the beach. After they finished, a wave ran up the beach and flowed over and around the sand turtle.

"Bye-bye, turtle," our daughter said as it disappeared under the wave. "He went back into the ocean," she informed her mother. It seemed like the natural thing for the turtle to do.

When we build a sand sculpture at the beach with our children or friends, we find pleasure in creating something, and being together. The joy does not depend on the permanence of the sand sculpture. We know the waves will rise and the sculpture will crumble. But that doesn't change the good times or the memories. The joy, the meaning, the satisfaction are in the *building*.

Fortunately, most things last longer than sand sculptures, and some things last for centuries. Michelangelo lived five hundred years ago, but many of his marble statues and paintings have survived and are still delighting and enriching us. We can visit cathedrals in Europe that were built eight hundred years ago, temples in Japan built twelve hundred years ago, and pyramids in Egypt built more than three thousand years ago. We also have ancient documents, codes, and religious writings that are thousands of years old. The Code of Hammurabi, the earliest legal code known in its entirety, dates back to Babylon sometime around 1750 B.C.

While some things have lasted for centuries, most of what we do will not last very long beyond our own lifetimes. In knowledge industries, what we contribute is soon superseded by the next discovery, the next truth, the next technological breakthrough. In organizational life, what we accomplish can fade quickly. We bring people together, build teams, and work toward our goals. When we leave the organization, we leave a legacy in the hearts and minds of the people who remain there, a legacy reflected in the culture of the organization. But as the years go by, only some of the legacy remains—and conditions can change dramatically in months instead of years.

We enjoy building
a sand castle,
even though it
will not last.
The joy is in
the *building*.

We had our moment in time. If it was meaningful, we have reason to be grateful.

What you spend years building may be destroyed overnight. But that doesn't change what you *accomplished*. You did something you can remember with pride and pleasure. Of course, it is gratifying when what you have built lasts far into the future. But don't forgo building just because it may not last. The joy and meaning that come with building *will* last. They will be yours forever.

> *What you spend years building may be destroyed overnight. Build anyway.*

The Ninth Commandment

People really need help but may attack
you if you do help them.
Help people anyway.

As a college student, I took a part-time job as a driver for
an elderly man. He was a man of accomplishment, a man who
had helped launch a major industry. He was intelligent and
his mind was alive, but he was trapped in a body that was no
longer working well. He found it difficult to walk and impos-
sible to climb stairs. His esophagus made it hard for him to
swallow and keep his food down. Sometimes he would throw
up while eating. It was not easy for him to shave or shower,
and he always looked unkempt. Sometimes there was an un-
pleasant odor about him.

It was my job to take him to the park, or to dinner, or
wherever he wanted to go. I learned to see the world in terms
of curbs, steps, ramps, and elevators. My job was to work
out his routes so that there would be no stairs. This was thirty
years ago, before federal law required ramps for people with
disabilities. I helped him in and out of the car, and gave him
my arm as he walked. I helped him over every curb and
every step. During meals, I had to be ready to clean up his
shirt, pants, and the table in front of him when he threw up
his food.

We got to be friends. I liked him, and I liked to hear about
his experiences. I was impressed with his accomplishments.
What was hard to accept was how upset he was with me all

the time. I wasn't doing the right thing to help him get out of the car; I was holding his arm too tight; I was holding his arm too loose. I picked the wrong place to enter the restaurant; the table was too close to a cold window; the food wasn't what he wanted. Week after week, outing after outing, I was always doing everything wrong. "Geez," I wanted to say, "I'm only trying to help." Sometimes, I had flashes of anger. But I kept quiet.

One day, while I waited for him to get ready to go to dinner, I tried to imagine what it was like being him. I tried to imagine what it was like to no longer be able to do things for oneself. Then it occurred to me that he wasn't irritated with me. He was irritated that he couldn't get out of the car on his own, and walk on his own, and climb stairs on his own, and eat without worrying about throwing up. He was upset with life, not with me. When I realized that, it all became easier. He didn't stop grumbling, but his grumbling stopped bothering me.

Most of us need help with one thing or another at one time or another. We need help learning how to do things, how to cope with problems, how to manage our time, our money, our lives. We need help with relationships, with decisions, with moral dilemmas. Nobody knows it all, or can do it all, alone. Knowing when we need help, and knowing where to find it, are basic to our survival and happiness.

Some people who need help deny that they need it. They don't want to face their inadequacies. Others who need help don't deny it, but they resent it. They don't want to be helpless or dependent; they don't want to appear ignorant. No-

Some people in need
have been betrayed
by others in the past.
They may be slow
to open up
and give you their trust.

body does. So even though their needs are obvious, when you try to help them, they may react negatively—even attack you for trying to help. They may be struggling with their pride, their self-image. They may not be able to acknowledge that they don't know what to do, or things aren't what they want them to be, or life isn't what it used to be.

Of course, it is possible to provide the wrong help, or to provide it the wrong way. We need to help others in ways that support their dignity and preserve their options. We need to be thoughtful in ascertaining if they need help, and if so, we need to learn what help is appropriate. We should never be condescending or domineering, just because we know they need our help. Some people in need have been betrayed or disappointed before and do not want to risk betrayal or disappointment again. They may be slow to open up and give you their trust.

If in doubt about whether a person is in need, think about the basics. People need food, clothing, and shelter. They need friends. They need meaningful activities. By observing, asking, and listening, you can identify needs and learn how best to meet them.

Everywhere you turn, there are people who really need help. If you help them, and they attack you, the attack may not be against you. They may be angry about their condition, or fighting against their feelings of helplessness or need. Don't let their attacks stop you. Others have helped you, over and over again. Now it's your turn. Enjoy the deep meaning that comes from assisting others in appropriate ways, and improving their quality of life.

People really need help but may attack you if you do help them. Help people anyway.

The Tenth Commandment

*Give the world the best you have and
you'll get kicked in the teeth.
Give the world the best you have anyway.*

In the classic western movie, *High Noon*, Gary Cooper played the role of Kane, a lawman who had brought peace and order to his town. After years of service, he decided to get married, take off his badge, and leave town. Minutes after his wedding ceremony, he received word that a gunman whom he had arrested years earlier had been let out of prison and would be arriving in town in less than two hours. Three of the gunman's cronies were waiting for him at the train station. They planned to join forces and walk down Main Street to kill Kane.

Kane decided to stay and fight. He put his badge back on and asked the men of the town to join him in the fight. They all declined. He was left to face the four gunmen alone.

The townspeople respected Kane, and many were grateful for his courage in bringing them peace for many years. He had given them his best. But now, in his time of need, they left him to be gunned down. He gave the town his best *anyway*. He stayed and fought the fight that had to be fought.

It is hard to judge what will happen when you give your best. You will probably be appreciated and supported. But giving your best may also result in a backlash of jealousy and rivalry. You may be accused of selfish ulterior motives; you may win false friends and true enemies; you may be shot down by small men and women with small minds; you may

The only thing
that costs more
than giving your best
is *not* giving your best.

witness the destruction of what you spent years building; you may be attacked by those you are helping; you may be left to fight the good fight alone.

The cost of giving your best can be high. The only thing that costs more is *not* giving your best. If you aren't giving your best, you aren't who you are supposed to be.

Never forget that you are unique. You are genetically unique, and you are unique in your combination of talent and experience. That means that you have something special to contribute. You make that contribution by giving the world your best.

Think about it. What kind of person doesn't give it his or her best? Why does anybody hold back? Why would anybody want to deliver a second-rate performance?

Certainly tact, strategy, and timing are important. You can look for the right opportunities, or *create* the right opportunities, to give your best. But even as you work to improve your skills so that you can do better in the future, there is always something that you can be doing that represents your best right now. Giving your best is not something you do later, it's something you do every day. You are already unique. You already have something to offer.

If you're not giving the world your best, what world are you saving it for? This is the life you are given. Your job is to make the most of it. It doesn't matter what the world does in response. Personal meaning comes from giving the world your best, no matter what.

Give the world the best you have and you'll get kicked in the teeth. Give the world the best you have anyway.

If you're *not*
giving the world
your best,
what world are
you saving
it for?

Part Three

Living the
Paradoxical Life

Living the
Paradoxical Life

If you accept the Paradoxical Commandments, you will find personal meaning in a crazy world. You will be free to live the paradoxical life.

Following the Paradoxical Commandments will help you to be the person you are really meant to be. You will be liberated from the things that are *not* the substance of life and do *not* satisfy. You will be focused on what is truly important and enriching.

The Paradoxical Commandments do not focus on popular symbols of success like wealth, power, and fame. Instead, they focus on meaning—the meaning you can get from loving others, doing good, being honest, thinking big, fighting for underdogs, building, helping others, and giving the world the best you've got. Each action you take can be enough, in and of itself, whether anything else follows from it. When you follow the Paradoxical Commandments, each action you take will be complete, because each action will bring its own meaning.

How do you live the paradoxical life? You do it by focusing on others and becoming part of something bigger than yourself. Love is focused on those who are loved. And joining in a cause, becoming part of an organization, or practic-

Each action you take
will be complete
because
each action
will bring its
own meaning.

ing a religion can give you the meaning that comes from being part of something bigger than yourself.

The meaning you need "inside" can be achieved by looking "outside"—to loving and helping others. The poet Emily Dickinson said more than a century ago:

> *If I can stop one Heart from breaking*
> *I shall not live in vain*
> *If I can ease one Life the Aching*
> *Or cool one Pain*
> *Or help one fainting Robin*
> *Unto his Nest again*
> *I shall not live in Vain.*

When you help others in both big and little ways, you know that you are not living in vain. Making a difference in the lives of others gives meaning to your own life.

There is really no other path to walk. When you understand that people have many needs, you have only three basic options:

(1) do nothing, and ignore the needs of others—an option that is a moral failure; or

(2) take advantage of people's weaknesses, cynically exploit their needs, and seek personal gain at their expense—an option that is an even worse moral failure; or

(3) do the right thing, and try to meet people's needs.

The third option is the only moral option. It is the only option that is based on love, and the only option that can gen-

You will find the most
personal meaning
when you focus on
others, and become
part of something
bigger than yourself.

erate hope. It is still the right option, even if you fail to achieve what you want to achieve.

If you try to do what is right and good and true, and feel that you have failed, you may be tempted to shift to the cynical option of exploiting others or the indifferent option of doing nothing. But there is no justification for falling into the two immoral options, just because things are not going the way you had hoped, or people don't appreciate what you have done for them.

We need results and should focus on getting them. When we get negative feedback, we should reconsider what we are doing. What did we learn? Should we do it differently next time? Are we really helping? Is there a better way to help? Would someone else be a better person to help? It is important to listen, observe, ponder, and make appropriate adjustments. But learning and adjusting are very different from giving up. You should not give up just because you weren't treated nicely or your efforts weren't as successful as you had hoped.

The issue of appreciation is a big one. Many of us feel that we are being taken for granted. The people we serve don't appreciate us, so why should we give them our best? The answer is that we have our own integrity and standards, and we derive meaning and satisfaction from doing a great job. It doesn't matter whether anybody knows or appreciates what we do—we still have to do what's right. We still have to be the best we can be. This is about us, not them. This is about how much *we* care, not about how much *they* care.

The desire to be appreciated is normal. But it is hard to

find meaning if one craves applause. A person who craves applause will focus on getting it, instead of focusing on meeting the needs of others. Also, people don't always remember to applaud. If you crave applause, your happiness will depend on the whims of others. By contrast, the meaning and satisfaction that you receive when you help others will always be yours, whether anybody else applauds or not.

This may seem very "saintly." However, living the paradoxical life is not about sainthood, it is about sanity. It is about the fact that applause and recognition do not provide as much meaning as loving and helping others. You shouldn't stop loving and helping others just because others don't seem to appreciate you.

The decision to lead the paradoxical life is a decision to be a certain kind of person. It may, in fact, be a decision to be *who you really a*re, or who you are really meant to be, rather than who society or your organization is pressing you to be. It's about your most cherished values, and how to live those values. It's about your integrity, your wholeness, your authenticity as a person.

It's also about your ability to stay the course. You will be able to love and help others better and longer if you take care of yourself first. Exercise regularly, eat right, get enough sleep. Take time to renew your spirit. Find new ways to grow, new ways to understand the world. And don't become over-burdened by accepting every cause or task that comes your way. Pick and choose; stay in balance. If you allow yourself to burn out, you will no longer have the energy to love and help others.

The paradoxical life

is not

about sainthood,

it is

about sanity.

I believe that each of us was born for a purpose, and immense meaning and satisfaction come from discovering and fulfilling that purpose. That purpose will be about making a difference for loved ones, friends, and community.

How do you make a difference? There are some very big problems to work on. War, starvation, disease, and environmental degradation are big problems. Crime, unemployment, racial discrimination, health care, substance abuse, and access to education are big problems.

People often find meaning by devoting themselves to issues that directly affect them or their families, friends, and neighbors. They work on problems that they just happen to come across, as in the biblical story of the Good Samaritan. The Samaritan came across a man who was beaten and robbed, lying by the side of the road. He took him to an inn and cared for him. The biblical tradition gives special attention to the needs of the poor, widows, and orphans.

Whether you act on needs that are big or small, long-term or immediate, near or far away, you can make a difference. You are most likely to make a difference if you address fundamental human needs. Those needs don't vary that much around the world. People need food, clothing, and shelter. They want good health, a safe environment, the opportunity to learn and grow, meaningful work, time with friends and family, a sense of belonging. People want dignity, peace, and justice.

There is great meaning to be found in helping others to meet their most fundamental needs. So do it. Work on world peace. Strive for justice. Protect the environment. Fight hun-

Each of us was born
for a purpose.
Immense meaning
and satisfaction
come from discovering
and fulfilling
that purpose.

ger and disease. Teach people how to read. Sing to a child. Mentor a teenager. Do something every day, and keep at it, day after day.

There is a wonderful story by Jean Giono entitled "The Man Who Planted Hope and Grew Happiness." The man in the story was a Frenchman who lived in southeastern France at the turn of the century. He lived alone in a barren area that had once been a forest with its own villages. His life was simple: He went out each day and planted trees. Year after year, decade after decade, seed by seed, he kept planting. The trees began to grow into a forest, which held water in the soil so that other plants could grow, and birds could make nests, and streams could flow, and families could return and build homes again. By the end of his lifetime, he had totally transformed and restored the natural environment of an entire region.

This is a good metaphor for a meaningful life: Work each day to plant hope and grow happiness for others. It is an especially good metaphor for the work of parents, guardians, and foster parents, helping their children day by day. The work may be simple and modest, yet powerful and long-lasting in its impact.

In the final analysis, who really has the most impact? Local, national, and international leaders have impact. But most of them have a small impact on many people, rather than a big impact on a few people. Parents, relatives, and friends can have a big impact on a few people, especially on children.

Nothing is more important than what happens to the children. If there is hope for our children, there is *every* hope. If there is no hope for our children, there is *no hope at all*. The

If there is hope
for our children
there is *every* hope.
If there is no hope
for our children,
there is *no hope at all.*

future of the world depends on the kinds of people today's children will turn out to be.

We all know that children need a lot of love and attention. Babies need lots of stimulation, and older children need lots of mentoring, and friendship. With the shift to single-parent families and two-parent families, both of whose parents work away from home, a lot of children are simply not getting the stimulation, mentoring, and friendship they need. The negative impacts can be large, and lifelong.

What we have learned in the past thirty years about the development of the brain is startling. When a baby is born, billions of neurons in the baby's brain are not yet programmed, and they connect to the circuits of the brain only in response to external stimuli. The richness and variety of the stimuli basically determine the structure and capabilities of the child's brain.

The things that make a positive difference in a child's development are things that all of us can do. All of us can hug or talk to or sing to or play with a baby. All of us can help a baby to touch and explore things of different sizes, shapes, colors, and textures. All of us can play music for a child, or take a child for a walk, or play catch with a child. What this means is that all of us can change lives, doing the simple, loving things that we all know how to do.

And it doesn't stop in early childhood. Researchers asked young people what they want, and many just wanted to spend more time with their parents or guardians or other caring adults. Two-thirds said they would like to spend more time with adults they can trust, who respect them.

In an age-segregated society, there aren't enough relationships between youth and adults. We can change that. Each young person needs at least one caring adult who will listen to her, teach her, encourage her, and celebrate accomplishments with her. Each of us can be a mentor and spend a few hours a week with a young person to help him or her to learn life skills, social competencies, and healthy attitudes that build resilience. Mentors, coaches, Sunday school teachers, and scout leaders are among the many adults who make a huge difference by giving their time, their wisdom, and their example to young people. We can be the caring adults who give hope to our youth and help them avoid major pitfalls.

When you live the paradoxical life, you find great personal meaning in loving and helping others. You can also find meaning by helping others to find meaning. Help others to learn what you have learned. Be the example they can follow in discovering and living their own paradoxical lives.

There is great hope in this. When more people are focused on meaning and less focused on "success," the world will start to make sense. People will pitch in to help, without worrying about who gets the credit. People will help each other, without worrying about who gets ahead in the company hierarchy. People will live their values and follow their hearts, and do the work they were born to do, even if it does not lead to power and wealth and prestige. Decisions will not be made on the basis of power rivalries, but on the basis of what is best for individuals, organizations, and society. People will not create problems to enhance their own power, but will solve problems to enhance their personal meaning. The world will

You can find meaning
by helping others
to find meaning.

be a lot less crazy when meaning-oriented individuals are out in front, addressing real needs and solving real problems without worrying about recognition or applause.

Whatever you choose to do, one thing is certain: When you live the paradoxical life, you will find personal meaning in a crazy world. You will make a difference. You will change lives.

One of the lives you change will be your own.

Dr. Kent M. Keith

Dr. Kent M. Keith was raised in six states. He has been an attorney, a state government official, a high-tech park developer, president of a private university, a graduate school lecturer, and a community organizer. He is currently vice president of the YMCA of Honolulu. He earned his B.A. from Harvard University, his M.A. from Oxford University, his certificate in Japanese from Waseda University, his law degree from the University of Hawaii, and his doctorate in education from the University of Southern California.

Dr. Keith has given and presented hundreds of speeches and conference papers on law, ocean technology, energy, economic development, secondary school activities, education, management, servant leadership, and the needs of youth. He is a Rhodes Scholar. In 1984 he was chosen as one of the Ten Outstanding Young Men of America by the United States Jaycees. In 1993 he was a University of Hawaii Distinguished Alumni awardee. He lives in Manoa Valley, Honolulu, with his wife, Elizabeth, and their three children, Kristina, Spencer, and Angela.

Dr. Keith is available for speaking engagements. He can be contacted at www.paradoxicalcommandments.com.